# FINDING THE
# FINISH LINE

Run your
Race for Him"

Andrea A. Clellis

# FINDING THE FINISH LINE

## NAVIGATING THE RACE OF LIFE THROUGH FAITH AND FITNESS

Andrea Cladis

CROSSLINK
PUBLISHING

# TABLE OF CONTENTS:

# PREFACE

## Finding the Finish Line—Closer to Christ

*"For the LORD God is a sun and shield; the LORD bestows favor and honor; no good thing does he withhold from those whose walk is blameless."*

*~ Psalm 84:11 ~*

re you ready to know Christ more? Are you ready to race for *His* grace? Join me on the rewarding journey towards developing an even closer relationship with Christ. Knowing that He alone is our sun and our shield, we are empowered to live our daily lives in eternal trust and reverence to Him. As such, we are called to walk as humble servants uplifting His kingdom and praising Him for His glory.

The purpose of this book is to explore God's enduring grace, His mercy, and more specifically, how faith, fitness, friendship, and consistent affirmations of self-worth enhance our overall physical and spiritual health, contributing to the experiential purpose of our everyday lives.

Where can you begin? Treat every day as though it were a race day! Not in the sense that you have an indeterminable will to be the best or be the fastest, but that you have an ongoing purpose. You have a goal and you have steadfast hope that in Christ alone the race would be a beautiful one. It would be glorious and lovely in each and every way. If you've ever competed in a race, you know the anxiety, the tension, the weeks and months of training you so desperately hope will pay off. There is fear, but there is also excitement and anticipation for an outcome yet unknown. And somehow that keeps us going. We are captivated by the mere mystery of it all, the challenge of the journey, and what is yet to come during the race. We cannot do it alone, though. We rely on the support of others, an internal drive towards personal success, and a need to have Christ with us through it all.

For to race without Christ? That's not racing at all. That's existing without living, that's breathing without taking in oxygen. That's the very epitome of wasting a life.

So live for Him. Race for Him. Run each day with purpose towards Him. For the finish line of life's still uncertain race will always remain in growing closer to Christ.

*"The Lord will work out his plans for my life—for your faithful love, O Lord, endures forever."*

*~ Psalm 138:8 ~*

# PART I: PREPARATION FOR THE RACE

## WAITING ON HIS TRUTH

*Defining Diligence in Faith*

*The truth is that no matter what I have in this world, nothing can replace the joy or love, the tears or elation, the memories or connection, the respite or the excitement that comes from human interaction—from being vulnerable enough to experience community in action, and to welcome the spontaneity that produces fulfillment in life.*

The pulsing issue of the past several years of my life has been balancing waiting on what I want in life while still seeking fulfillment in Christ. At twenty-five years old, in the midst of a daily litany of questioning and subsequent confusion, I realized just how much I had been struggling with what God had destined for me and how He was presently using me to fulfill His purpose for my life. According to my playbook and script for life, twenty-five years old ended up looking much different than I envisioned it would be. As I foresaw my life, prior to the defining decade of the 20s, I thought twenty-five meant finding love, getting married, completing my master's degree, moving to another state, having a well-paying job (preferably in writing), and serving others with my talents. Some of these things have come to fruition, but most of them remain wishful thinking—or as C.S. Lewis likes to say, "thoughtful wishing." I prefer the latter phrase. And instead of my fanciful list of wants for twenty-five, I'm twenty-eight now and currently not married, though I have discovered love, I have held various writing jobs (none that have paid well) and, after college, earned a teaching degree despite the holistic recognition that I never wanted to be a teacher! I have read more books than I can count. I have overcome anorexia. I have published writing in literary journals. I work as a high school English teacher, Sunday school teacher, and group fitness instructor. I became a licensed health coach. I have competed in triathlons. I am training for another marathon. I moved back home. I am still living in the same state. I quit my first teaching job, but continued to pursue that path for my life. It sounds like I am fulfilled; I am busy; my life is full, right? But regardless of my desire to keep moving forward in whatever capacity I can, I still feel utterly, shamefully lost in life. But, whom am I to blame for this feeling of dissatisfaction? Is selfish ambition and consistent planning a sin of unworthy cause or of lost faith? Am I a sinner for desiring that which I can't have? For standing akimbo and looking at life with a smarmy smirk on my face? Mayhap, I believe—yes. Yes. I am. We all are.

I plan, plan, plan, and things never work out the way *I would* like. So, it becomes necessary to step back, remove myself from selfish ways and ask, "What are the sacred plans *He* has for me?" As I contemplated my version of a contrived "twenty-five-year-old" reality, I have realized that my original "plan" (notice the short list) does not even mention Christ. And this is the junction wherein I encountered the first problem. My perspective growing up was one in which Christ was my friend, my redeemer; HE brought me joy; HE created me; HE saved me through grace. So, naturally I have been wondering why my original high-school generated vision of "twenty-five" does not even mention Christ. Was I under the assumption that by age twenty-five I would not need Him anymore? He was never planning to abandon me, but was I planning to abandon Him?

Reflecting on this reality now, I have grown to recognize it is absolutely imperative to realize that the most important thing in the consideration of goals, dreams, and visions at any age should first and foremost be improving upon our relationship with Christ. To want to know HIM more and to be doing everything we can do ensure that happens. *What if my only intent for twenty-five was to be so enamored with Christ—with a trust so profound that a list need not be made? How incredible would that have been?* And how incredible would it be if the next time someone asks where I would like to be in ten years, my simple, limpid response was, "Closer to Christ." **Closer to Christ**. Repeat that phrase. The simple phrase relieves stress, nullifies tension, soothes worry, and produces an overwhelming sense of calm. Thus, I believe that "closer to Christ" also translates to closer to where we would like to be in our heart and in our lives. As author Carol Kent aptly explains, "God created us with an overwhelming desire to soar…. He designed us to be tremendously productive and to mount up with wings like eagles, realistically dreaming of what He can do with our potential."

Since I have had some unforeseen disappointments in life leaving me clouded by anxiety, fear, and unrest, I have been gifted with the time to come to know God in a way I never knew was possible. Patience is a difficult feat, especially for Type A people who equate hard work with success and consistently crave the most desirable outcomes. But what if God's success in my life is not the kind of success I envision? How can I be sure that what I do with my life is honoring and pleasing to Him? Is my work done to the glory of His name? Through serving others, I have come to embrace humility and, through giving of myself for others, I have come to receive palpable peace. Yes, peace in the present moment. Peace in the past. Peace for the future. Right now it absolutely feels as though I were playing the waiting game of life. I am riding the stationary bike to nowhere, but my legs are becoming stronger every day. I can't see the finish line, but I have found my stride. My grip has tightened. My endurance has increased; my thoughts have produced clarity, and God's not only pedaling beside me, but He is also in front of me and behind me. His ambient presence is known and, through this waiting period as with all others I have endured in life, He is using me towards growing in His purpose.

*Remember: to wait, Biblically speaking, is not to assume the worst, worry, fret, make demands, or take control. Nor is waiting inactivity. It is a sustained effort to stay focused on God through prayer and belief. To wait is to "rest in the Lord and wait patiently for Him" (Psalm 37:7). So, delight yourself in God and He will bring rest to your soul. For God is at work in each of us, whether we know it or not, whether we want it or not.*

"God works out everything in conformity
with the purpose of his will."

Ephesians 1:11

~~~~~~~~~~~~~~~~~~~~~~~~~~~~~~~~~~~~~~~~~~~~~

# MAKE A PLAN FIT FOR CHRIST
*Training Mind, Body, and Spirit*

**Refuge in the Unknown**

In life we are uncertain of where this winding path may lead –
Long or short, wide or narrow,
It beckons us; we plead.

We cannot know what the next turn holds,
No matter how careful our plans –
God's story unfolds before us; the mystery lies in His hands.

Yet luckily for us, He gave us grace in provision –
The presence of those who take us by the hand,
To wipe a tear or quell a fear so alone we do not stand.
For whether long or short, curved or straight, uncertainty still be our guide –
Content for each passing moment because His love surrounds its every side.

The challenge of twenty-five years-old, or any age for that matter, is not simply to yearn for the things you think you should be doing or those tangible and intangible things you may desire to have, but to *stay focused on God*. In the same way that I stay focused on a fitness regimen and training plan *every single day*, I must work to keep my focus in sync with my heart's desire for Christ. Keep in mind: when you train, you're training for a race that you have yet to begin. The finish line of the race has not yet been drawn. You're building strength for the test with an outcome you can't fully control. Personally, if I can make the time to run, bike, swim, lift, eat, sleep, repeat…I can most certainly make the time to kneel—and yes, I mean kneel— to pray. I am not saying that prayer cannot be done at any time or from anywhere, but a conscious effort to take the time to assume a reverent position should be part of every day. If you can stand up to run, you can kneel down to pray and spend time with God.

Making a plan fit for Christ means balancing the discipline of intentionality in faith with that of structure towards attaining purpose in life. Being fit for a race requires planning with careful attention to physical training, nutritional needs, continued education in training methods, practicing with a team or receiving coaching to improve technique, and creating ample time for rest and recovery. Likewise, being fit for Christ requires planning with careful attention to caring for your body in ways that honor God, regular prayer and conversation with God, active participation in your church community, wisely seeking counsel from other Christians, dedicated commitment to living out your faith through acts of service to others, spreading the Gospel, and daily acting in obedience to His will.

Consequently, through adapting to a lifestyle of fitness in your faith, you will not only be able to more clearly discern Christ's purpose for your life, but you will also develop stamina to stay the course, avoid temptations, openly accept grace, and bring others into the community of Christ. Maintaining high levels of both physical fitness and fitness in faith requires consistent effort and conscientious work.

But the journey to become closer to Christ is far worthier than any other experience you will have in your life. It is an all-encompassing, life-giving venture towards a finish line of redemptive love, promise, salvation, and eternal life.

*"We have this hope as an anchor for the soul, firm and secure. It enters the inner sanctuary behind the curtain."*

Hebrews 6:19

# BE VIBRANT

*Living in the Present Moment*

The blessing of good health, a deep connection to community, the power of selfless creativity, and learning to live in the present: what serving others as a fitness trainer has engendered within me.

## Why it "fits" to be present

Recently, I commemorated a five-year anniversary since I first became a licensed, accredited group exercise instructor, and seven years since I first dabbled in the health and wellness industry by taking a leap of faith and becoming a certified Zumba fitness instructor.

It has been a unique journey for me that has taken interesting turns and led to unexpected success. It has been a time in my life—aside from everything else going on, from finishing schooling to taking on postgraduate degrees, and commencing full-time jobs—wherein I have learned, grown as a person, discovered strengths and self-confidence I never knew I had, and fully risked, for the first time in my life, the reward of true investment in something that mattered to me, without the need or concern for only pleasing others.

Becoming a fitness instructor has been the one thing I have done most consistently in terms of employment in my life and by far has been the work, even trumping working as a magazine columnist, that has brought the most satisfaction and gratitude to my life. However, if you had asked me ten years ago what I wanted to do with my life, teaching fitness was not even an idea of mine or a speck on the radar. And trust me, with that Type A personality, I had plans, goals, and avenues for my life set out to follow. Yet, as I preach in fitness classes—fostering a foundation of flexibility and stretching yourself outside of your comfort zone is what yields the greatest results. I suppose that applies to life, too. Be flexible. Be spunky. Be on point. Be fit! Get after it!

## Beginning to Live Fit

My interest in fitness has grown throughout the course of my life, but first became a sincere passion of mine during college as I was desperately working to recover from an eating disorder that nearly claimed my life.

I grew up in an athletic family and spent much of my childhood as an athlete, so staying active has always been important to me. I competitively played tennis, soccer, softball, basketball, and I was a swimmer and dancer. I was never an elite athlete or a star player in any of the sports I chose, but I loved learning new skills, moving my body, and engaging my competitive nature in a healthy way by channeling that fire within me through sporting events, matches, and competitions.

Up until my freshman year of high school, I remained physically active and maintained a healthy body. It was something I never thought much about and therefore easily took for granted. However, as pressures mounted in high school ranging from changing family dynamics to the death of grandparents and pets along with overwhelming social, academic, personal, and peer pressures, I became withdrawn, anxious, and depressed. Unfortunately, this led to a severe eating disorder that negatively impacted much of my high school experience. As my body slowly deteriorated from lack of proper nourishment, I gradually became unable to participate in sports—and life in general—in the way I always had. I will never forget the day I was told I was no longer allowed to exercise or workout. I thought my life was over. I was benched from the tennis team, swim team, and even had to sit out from gym class. It was humiliating for me, but I was not strong enough to keep up anymore. Yet working out—something that had always been an outlet for me; a release for my stress and anxiety—was being stripped from me in hopes that my body could have time to catch up with itself and to heal.

I remember how much it hurt to walk up a flight of stairs, or how I could barely lift my backpack, or how many layers of clothing I would wear in desperate efforts to stay warm, or even how my swimsuit was loose on my once muscular. I remember clumps of hair falling out, the translucence of my skin, the sunken eye sockets on my face, and bloody gums with the constant seeping taste of iron in my mouth, and feeling of cotton constantly lining my throat. It was a struggle I will not ever forget, but through the pain I learned never again to take my health for granted. As I wrestled each day and my weight continually dwindled to a mere 60 pounds, I feared that I would never again be able to think clearly about things, that I would never be able to exercise, that I would never have the strength again to play sports, or to lace up my running shoes, or even to simply dance around the house.

As I bungled along into senior year, fearless prayer, devotion to faith, steadfast support from family, and counseling that I fought going to, I eventually had a change of attitude and developed a newfound desire to become healthy again—no matter what the cost. Once I was ready to embrace the arduous road to mental and physical recovery, I recognized that I had something to live for. The turning point for me was the ever powerful reminder that I had a Creator who made me in His image and He had not forsaken me. He had blessed me with life! I needed to honor that gift to glorify Him and know that just as my family never left my side through hardship, He would be there healing my hurt, ameliorating my pain, and guiding my steps. I primarily credit my sister, Stacey, for reminding me each and every day that God's love endures, protects, and is always, always worth living for. She was and remains to be the sheer embodiment of Christ in my life. I love her beyond words, and for her self-sacrificing, unconditional love that saved my life, I owe her my deepest gratitude.

**Progressively Improving**

During my first few years of college I still struggled periodically with my eating disorder, but was able to find self-confidence again, a sense of purpose, vitality, and the depth of knowing self-worth. During my junior year after reigniting my love of dance through Zumba fitness classes, I decided to acquire my official Zumba licensure. This was my first experience of turning passion into action, and it was memorable because it happened during my final year with my last surviving grandparent, my Greek grandmother, Yia-Yia. She had always encouraged my love of dance and education, and one of the fondest memories I have is that I picked her up on my way home from the all-day Zumba training I had attended in Chicago and spent an hour trying to explain "Zumba" to no avail. It's not quite like 'Zorba' Greek dancing, which she knew well, but it was dancing nonetheless! I remember her laughing and telling me it was "interesting" and that she thought I could "Zooombah" my way back to a physically healthier state. As always, Yia-Yia ended up being right about that and pretty much everything else in my life. I still miss her dearly.

Experiencing a positive change in my physical health led to great success from grades to friendships, to school involvement, scholarships, high honors, being a senior-of-the-year finalist, sorority founder, and more. I graduated from college in 2011 entering the field of journalism. However, through several internships, trials and career searches in that field, I decided to take advice and pursue postgraduate schooling to acquire my secondary education licensure to teach high school English. While pursuing this degree, one of the requirements was that I had to take a kinesiology course. Bemoaning a science class, my least favorite subject, this class ultimately ended up being a game-changer for me. Yes, I was teaching Zumba at the time, but this course sparked a new conscious interest in health and wellness for me, and exposed me to the many ways in which I could share my passions and talents with others. As I am often reminded by my life verse, Proverbs 19:21, "Many are the plans in a man's heart, but it is the Lord's purpose that prevails."

While my focus remained on finishing my education degree, it was not too long after taking that kinesiology class that I researched personal training, group exercise, and the steps I needed to take to become an exercise leader or instructor. As a result, I studied to become an American Council on Exercise group fitness instructor, began teaching classes, and through continuing education, have added specialties in areas such as Barre, H.I.I.T (High Intensity Interval Training), Kickboxing, Pilates, and Spin. It still surprises me that most of the time we are habitually unaware of when God is working in us, through us, or charting the course He intended for our lives.

Taking the risk to go after these things was one of the best decisions of my life and turned out to be a perfect fit for me. Combining my love of wellness and exercise with teaching, helping others, and promoting a healthy, fit body image rather than a thin one plagued by the trauma of anorexia was, and still is, cathartic and empowering for me.

## Becoming Fully Present

Through my experiences teaching fitness thus far, one of the most meaningful things I have learned is that BEING PRESENT in the moment is the surest way to find happiness. Being present in any given moment means fully surrendering yourself to the notion of lost time and space. A moment can seemingly last an eternity if you allow it to. Consider the first time you were kissed, welcomed an embrace from a loved one after a long-awaited homecoming, or when you ate a most scrumptious meal that tantalized your mouth in a sensory overload of textures and flavors. Consider what it feels like to be onstage, pass an important test, go on a long drive and lose track of sights, sounds, landmarks, passing cars, the feeling of becoming one with the very effervescence of time that catapults thoughts towards motion and motion into action. It is when the every-ready grind of time is momentarily lost in the melancholy bliss of what is right here and right now.

When I maintain a positive energy about my being, set aside worries and anxieties, or rid myself of concerns about past mistakes or future plans, I become authentically mindful in a way that allows me to fully give of myself to others. This is required for good fitness classes to become great ones, for excellence to trump mediocrity, and for enjoyment in life to reach its quintessence.

Through fitness, prayer, and writing, I have honed my ability to not just be present in a particular moment (as in just "showing up") but also to be FULLY present. This means that I am only absorbed in the present motion of what I am doing within the scope of the specific class I am teaching. I am paying attention to musical beats, rhythms, my body's movement and form, the participants in class, breathing patterns, expectations and individual objectives for my clients. If I fail to fully tune into the responsibilities of the environment for myself, I will not be successful. It is imperative for me to completely engage and let go of everything outside of the studio. There must not be thought of the past, trials of the day and/or plans for after class or even for the next class. When I am able to consciously and subconsciously feel my body move, taste my sweat, and light up with a smile that breeds a mix of joy and consternation on the faces of participants, everything else fades away. Then, when I glance in the mirror at everyone standing behind me, I pause subtly—sometimes losing my count and place in the music—to soak in the joy I observe being produced in the space of the moment. It tingles the core of my being. The other work will wait. Life will still be there when class has ended, but when you realize living is what happens right here and right now in the very spaces we so quickly shun—that is when our attitude changes and we come alive. That is when the real living of life comes to fruition. It is where we ultimately find ourselves finding life.

**Finding Your Moment**

I've always had a stubborn, determined, and orderly personality. I want to have fun, but at the same time I have an affinity for planning and a desire to control things, making sure I have crossed all my "T's" and dotted all my "I's." I was the overly involved, nerdy student in college with straight A's who would study on Friday nights and get semester projects done within the first few weeks of classes.

I have been known to take on more than I can handle or set unrealistic standards or expectations for myself and others. It's a strength and a weakness for me, but being involved in fitness has changed both my perspective and demeanor towards everyday life.

There's a regimen to fitness I enjoy, such as training for a race or preparing a specific class format, but more so, I love the freedom that fitness brings. The learning to live with mistakes, the idea that things won't be perfect on the first try or even ever, that I can't control everything, and aside from being early for classes, planning and prepping isn't always consistent and that's okay! Granted, there are good days and bad days, but I like to make use of the popular cliché as I relay to those I train that, "You'll always regret the workout you didn't do."

It is the sweaty smiles, feelings of victory, accomplishment, the one extra rep someone couldn't do merely a few days ago, the progressive improvements, and enhanced self-confidence people develop in all areas of their life when they slow down enough to take time to authentically care for themselves—that's when all the combined moments begin to show their worth.

**Remembering to Cool Down**

Lastly, every fitness class must have a cool down of some kind. This is the time where participants take that break to relish in the work they've just done as their heart rate returns to a steady state, sweat glistens ever-so-gently from their brow, and they breathe deep breaths of victory. Paying close attention to the connection between the body and mind while allowing them to work together harmoniously breeds an element of wholeness and stillness that translates into better management of our busy lives. During the cool down, I am reminded to slow down, to pay attention, and not to rush. If a stretch is rushed, its effective purpose is essentially lost, and the mood of the class will hurriedly stagnate. So, take that pause each day to cool down and to find that synchronous satisfaction of mind and body within that momentary reward earned for a job and work well done!

## Jumping Rope One Hop at a Time

Perhaps I have consumed far too many kale smoothies, of course balanced out by post-workout cravings for chocolate or cupcakes with extra frosting. And maybe I have competed in far too many recreational races; I have stressed myself out, worn myself bare, tried to support myself through multiple jobs both within and outside of fitness; I have suffered overuse injuries on a monthly basis and have hit the wall of burnout like anyone else.

BUT, despite all that, when it comes to my work as a fitness instructor, I'm still jumping rope! One hop at a time, day by day I am staying on my toes jumping through the rope(s) of life. And even when my legs get tired or my eyes grow weary, I am still smiling every time I learn something new, choreograph a funky, fresh dance, stretch my own limits of growth in fitness, and make a concerted effort towards improving myself and others.

There is magic in the moment when I strap on that microphone headset, bust out some exciting music, and watch a room fill up with people anxious to spend an hour of their day with me. Whether it is 6:00 AM or 6:00 PM, I absolutely love it. That's MY moment.

So go find your moment.

Live it.

Love it.

Be fully PRESENT within it.

*"He gives strength to the weary and increase the power of the weak. Even youths grow tired and weary, and young*

*men stumble and fall; but those who hope in the Lord will renew their strength. They will soar on wings like eagles; they will run and not grow weary; they will walk and not be faint."*

Isaiah 40:29-31

~~~~~~~~~~~~~~~~~~~~~~~~~~~~~~~~~~~~~~~~~~~~~~

# STAY FOCUSED

*Sheltered by the Under Armor of God*

*Finally, be strong in the Lord and in his mighty power. Put on the full armor of God, so that you can take your stand against the devil's schemes. For our struggle is not against flesh and blood, but against the rulers, against the authorities, against the powers of this dark world and against the spiritual forces of evil in the heavenly realms. Therefore put on the full armor of God, so that when the day of evil comes, you may be able to stand your ground, and after you have done everything, to stand. Stand firm then, with the belt of truth buckled around your waist, with the breastplate of righteousness in place, and with your feet fitted with the readiness that comes from the gospel of peace. In addition to all this, take up the shield of faith, with which you can extinguish all the flaming arrows of the evil one. Take the helmet of salvation and the sword of the Spirit, which is the word of God.*

~ Ephesians 6:10-18 ~

**Relentless in Lent, Selfish in Fast**

"I've lost my focus. I can't even think straight anymore," I went on, berating a litany of my personal shortcomings in a FaceTime conversation with a good friend of mine serving on Mercy Ships in Madagascar.

"I think you need to let it be and let it go," he chided me. "If one night you've hit your groove, march with it. If another night the vessel is empty, go sail your ship elsewhere and leave the pen on the table. Not to say it's not good to pace yourself, just let the story unveil itself as it's ready. It's not about being the hero of now, it's about consistently acknowledging failures and embracing the gift of grace."

After all, why am I not racing *for His grace* rather than running from it?

**Accountability. Credibility. Intentionality.**

These are all things that Christians should be striving towards as they seek to live out their lives as disciples of the Lord. However, when was the last time you asked yourself, "What did I do for Christ today? How I am serving to further His Kingdom today?" Maybe you consciously ask yourself questions such as these on a regular basis, but for the majority of people, it is evident we consistently fall short of doing so—or even in so doing, following through with what we know and believe to be right.

In the Christian life, when it comes to armor and focus, I often think of Lent—a deeply important time of prayer, reflection, meditation, and renewal. During Lent, as we prepare for the Resurrection of Christ, we are given the opportunity to strengthen our faith, renew our beliefs, and **intentionally** focus on the way in which we emulate

Christ in our daily lives. Often we get caught up in Christian cultural doctrines of fasting, giving things up, or being repentant to Christ as a trade for bettering our relationship with Christ or painfully honing our focus on things above. Yet, at what point do these practices simply become practices to feel good or better ourselves versus **credibly** improving ourselves through Him?

Let's take fasting as the most obvious example of this practice, beginning with the most common form of fasting which is fasting from food.

Certainly, we can fast from bad behaviors or habits, but when we fast from food—per church tradition or through our own allotted choice, why are we doing it? What I have commonly observed in the past is that we choose to relinquish ourselves during Lent initially in the sense of "I should do this," "I have to do this," or "this will serve to restore my faith." However, do we ever see those things through? Often, it occurs that many people merely use fasting for personal gain rather than preparing their hearts for the Lord. And this is the exact opposite purpose of the fast. Let's say you give up desserts— or chocolate—or adopt a mild starvation diet on certain days. And while your hunger pains dwindle as the weeks pass, does your mind gather its burdened thoughts on Christ? Or do you end up thinking, *Well, hey—look, I lost a few pounds! Great. Oh, and thanks God?*

This is where the problem sets in. What you're doing is no longer being done for the glory of Christ. It's being done to attain selfish ends, when during Lent we should reflect alone on Christ's selfless example of suffering. Don't diet and call it fasting for Christ. Don't give up swearing and say, "Oh, look, people have more respect for me now." Don't fast without intention. And don't live without **accountability** in your faith. Lean on others, lean on the church, and most of all, lean on Christ in all things.

I'm not here to discourage fasting if it's something that works for you and allows you to hone your focus in a productive way for Christ. But I am providing a challenge to consider another way to live out days of Lent or fasting. View it as an opportunity rather than a self-sacrificial burden. As always, Lent is a season of breaking down as we stand awaiting affirmation of the greatest mystery and miracle mankind has ever known.

So perhaps as you approach this Lenten season of your life, take time to change your focus. Instead of a distracted, Church-appropriated or personal fast, why not consider what you can do each day to give of yourself—to fast from your selfishness into selflessness?

To be inclusive.

To serve others.

To seek to further Christ and His kingdom.

Giving up self is the greatest gift we can give in this world. And quite often it can be a much more difficult task than merely giving up that chocolate bar at the end of the day.

What will result, however, is a lasting way of life. It is a withdrawing from self and a drawing into the investment of others. Spreading the Gospel, making time, giving of self in ways you've never done. Let the "I" become a "we" and the "me" become a "what" does "He" need from me.

My charge for your life is to act upon these things not only in Lent, but in your everyday walk of faith. To fast from self. To give to others. To live for Him. To be entirely relentless in your attitudes and actions so that you may become entirely selfless, humble servants, and reverent Disciples of Christ!

*"Your love has given me great joy and encouragement, because you, brother, have refreshed the hearts of the Lord's people."*

Philemon 7

~~~~~~~~~~~~~~~~~~~~~~~~~~~~~~~~~~~~~~~~~~~~

# PART II: RUNNING YOUR RACE

## RACE DAY

*Running in Christ Alone*

*"Therefore I do not run like someone running aimlessly; I do not fight like a boxer beating the air. No, I strike a blow to my body and make it my slave so that after I have preached to others, I myself will not be disqualified for the prize."*

1 Corinthians 9:26-27

The clock. That smite. That tasteless, vain despot. TIME: The sword of life's existence. The liberator and the prison guard. The watch and the bell. The clock.

Twisted braids tightly caressed her neck, falling past the name on her grass-stained red-and-gold running tee. Sweat pulsed at her temples, bled down into her stained, breathless cheeks. The clock read 2 hours, 45 minutes. Her heart felt heavy and her willpower wavered. Her soul rushed backwards. She had four miles yet to run and her blistered feet winced for relief. Time ticked. It's just a race, *she thought.* It's only me against myself.

*One jettisoned step too late she crossed that finish line. Propelled by friends and fans she intentionally collapsed, then blacked out, evaded all sense of self-pressure and aggravated, perpetual doubt.*

*There wouldn't be another race if she never had to face another morning. Never enough. She felt she would never be enough.*

*She had trained perfectly. Honed her focus on eating well, being the deserving athlete she knew she was. But failure stung like poison. Motivation waned like rising crime rates. "Run your race," the refrain beckoned. "Run your race!"*

The purpose of this anecdote is to demonstrate that no matter what the race—a marathon, chasing a job, a dream, a life—it isn't going to be easy. There are going to be blistered feet and pestering thoughts of self-doubt. There will be failure and there will be success. There will be moments where existing seems the only option and living, a secondary afterthought. There will be spaces and seasons in the race of life that go by too quickly, while others pass too slowly. Yes, it's going to be hard. Each day will not produce a smile, but on that race day, the morning you wake up, look up, talk to God, pray, lace up those shoelaces and prepare yourself for the race of your life. God has given you the gift of living a beautiful life, racing an unchartered course that only He can see.

*"Let us not become weary in doing good, for at the proper time we will reap a harvest if we do not give up."*

*~ Galatians 6:9 ~*

~~~~~~~~~~~~~~~~~~~~~~~~~~~~~~~~~~~~~~~~~~~~~

# MY WEARINESS AMAZES ME
*Thanking Bob Dylan*

One of Bob Dylan's most popular songs, "Mr. Tambourine Man," contains one of my favorite lyrics of all time. It's a lyric that I've always been able to relate to and one that I think we all experience from time to time amidst the hardship, the day-to-day schedules, and the ominous demands of our lives. As Dylan sings about the rhythms of life both in its beauty and its sadness he says, "My weariness amazes me; I'm branded on my feet … I have no one to meet and the ancient street's too dead for dreaming. Yes, to dance beneath the diamond sky with one hand waving free, silhouetted by the sea, circled by the circus sands with all memory and fate driven beneath the waves. Let me forget about today until tomorrow."

There are times when we all grow weary; we are branded on our feet and we feel paralyzed in the crypt of slowly passing time. But when that happens, we have to stop and give ourselves permission to step back, recharge, and find a renewal of purpose.

BREATHE.

PAUSE.

LEARN.

THINK.

Enjoy the moment.

Yes, I'm saying that! My everlasting mind of hyphenated hypocrisy strikes once again. I'm reminding myself to take a pause to discover those margins of life where living fosters activity, dreams become reality, and feelings ignite passion.

Surely—a pause. A moment. A break. A rest. Where can these precious things find their place in my life? I'm still trying to figure that one out, but I'm growing through the process. Since I've added to my busy life through teaching high school English classes, my life has been a nonstop, day-to-day adventure and journey of work and excitement. From curriculum planning and grading to meeting new people, traveling to new places, seeing new faces—it has been a stressful experience of highs and lows, ups and downs, and pour-over-my-soul exhaustion. Yet, at the same time, it's been a marvelous blessing! To know I'm living a life so full of God's love, his grace, and his enduring mercy is an indescribable feeling!

Even though teaching high school may not be a consummate dream of mine, I am humbled by the opportunity to teach and help foster the growth of intriguing young adults. They are each unique, individual children of God! I am in a community that believes the reason and purpose behind all things is worthy. Regardless of how long and tiring each day may be and no matter how trivial each task may seem, every last nuance has value to God. Yes, there are days when "my weariness amazes me," but all that matters is that we trust in His timing, His plan, and His script for our lives.

Adopting and fully embracing the life of a servant-leader means giving of self for others with dignity, grace, respect, and compassion. It means not questioning the affliction of the moment but accepting its worth. In order to lead most effectively, I'm learning that who I am and all I will be is measured most consistently by what I've selflessly shared of my talents and what I've given to others, not what I've done for myself. It means being a servant in the likeness of Christ—growing tired, but finding renewal. For me, being enveloped in the uncommon community found amongst Christ's followers at home, where the example of my father is what I desire for my children someday, at Church, and now at work, provides assurance for hope, grace for belief, and faithfulness to abound in all things.

Am I tired? Yes. Weary? Of course. Do I find myself confused and overwhelmed nearly every day? Absolutely. But I am content with me, with who I am, what I am, and all I will become. I wake up each morning to the song, "For your glory, for your kingdom, for your name, oh Lord—HERE I am" (lyrics by Tommy Walker, 2002). It's an empowering reminder that each day is a gift to be lived to and for the glory of God. Being present in Christ, in his ubiquitous mercy, to commence each day means I'm living the wholeness he desires for me. Self comes second. HE comes first.

*"I will remain confident of this: I will see the goodness of the Lord in the land of the living. Wait for the Lord; be strong and take heart and wait for the Lord."*

Psalm 27:13-14

~~~~~~~~~~~~~~~~~~~~~~~~~~~~~~~~~~~~~~~~~~~~~~~~~

# SWEAT AND TEARS; ANGST AND FEARS

*Running the Race for Christ*

**To everything there is a season,
and a time to every purpose under heaven:**

*A time to be born, and a time to die; a time to plant, and a time to pluck up that which is planted; a time to kill, and a time to heal; a time to break down, and a time to build up; a time to weep, and a time to laugh; a time to mourn, and a time to dance; a time to cast away stones, and a time to gather stones together; a time to embrace, and a time to refrain from embracing; a time to get, and a time to lose; a time to keep, and a time to cast away; a time to rend, and a time to sew; a time to keep silence, and a time to speak; a time to love, and a time to hate; a time of war, and a time of peace (Ecclesiastes 3: 1–8).*

To find the finish line, you first have to see the starting line. You have to feel that anticipation to begin and use that stored fuel to propel you onward through a race.

During a very difficult point in my life, after resigning from one of my first full-time jobs, I felt useless, hopeless, distant, and each day was consumed with regret. About a month after I had resigned, I knew I had made it past the starting line of a new chapter in my life, but my body was weary and my mind completely numb. If you've ever gone for a run in hot weather, after a certain point you know the feeling of numb legs and tingling toes. Yet, whether you recognize it or not in the moment, sometimes the bliss comes when countless miles have been treaded, but you can no longer keep up with them. Your body feels an endless stride and your mind a limitless, selfish pride.

But what happens when your legs stop moving? Take unemployment, for example, and the effect it might have on a person:

Day 1 (of unemployment): Relief, rest, solace.

Day 2: Feelings of comfort, belief that you will be okay!

Day 3–10: I'm getting antsy, scared, bored, and I need rest.

Day 11 – Day 30: I'm feeling paralyzed; what's next, get me out of my life, I'm crawling out of my skin. I can't focus. I feel trapped. Anything. I want out!

There's a slow deterioration that happens to a mind or body at rest. While renewal is what's expected, atrophy is what sets in. Lacking any tangible work, focus or purpose to hold onto and being suffocated by a world filled with meaningless anecdotes and the archived annoyance of recycled themes and worry, a resting mind or body is a failing one. To know all that one is capable of but also to sit on a precipice of misunderstanding and unsure footing is perhaps the most soul-sucking, gut-wrenching feeling in the world.

It seems most obvious—just go out and do things, right? Do things in the way you have always done, but what if suddenly you cannot? Suddenly you're a sunken, energy-less frame of a has-been, used-to-be, and does anyone still see me?

So, you retreat. You want to retreat and disappear for the very comfort and silence of being alone. The people, the noise, the drone—make it all go away. People exhaust. Friends may encourage, but you push them away. Streaming thoughts of unworthiness echo in every chamber of your mind. You fight. You scream. You cry. Rejection. Failure. Get up. Fall down. Try, try, try again. No. No. No. Apathy. Loss. Anger. Doubt—ever creeping doubt. Seething villainous cries for help—get me out!

An engine without a spark.

A muse without a tale.

A heart without a pulse.

A life with no avail.

A roller coaster of fear. A crippling wave that greets every morning and cries out—do more, be more, wake up—get out! Live life. But sometimes you won't be able to find it. The wave washes over you from one day to the next, and you become a weathered shore waiting for the tide to pass, the night to settle, the wave to come again. You become consumed with angst and fears, sweat and tears.

Perhaps you seek everything but grasp onto nothing. Decoding the feigned myth of success, trapped by a paralyzing world, weighted down with duress.

There remains a constant, though—through training, through life, through every high and every low, there is redemption for our hearts. Know that God is good. Believe that His mercy is everlasting. Accept that you won't understand the challenges, but praise Him for allowing you to share in the suffering of Christ. If you have the gift to feel so deeply that your soul aches, your chest quakes, and your sight is not always clear, praise Him more! Keep your eye on the prize so that despite all earthly yearnings, wants, and concerns, you still keep your heart focused to welcome His presence in all things and to fully embrace His eternal grace and mercy. When you catch yourself looking down, start looking up. Look to HIM. Run *your* race for Christ.

*"He has shown you, O mortal, what is good. And what does the Lord require of you? To act justly and to love mercy and to walk humbly with your God."*

Micah 6:8

~~~~~~~~~~~~~~~~~~~~~~~~~~~~~~~~~~~~~~~~~~~~~

# PERSEVERANCE IN IDENTITY
## Finding the Authentic Self

**Social Judgment Theory** *is based on the idea that individuals make judgments based upon experiences and beliefs from their past. When people are introduced to a persuasive message, their beliefs will influence how they perceive the message and will ultimately determine if they should accept a* *new position or not. Should they change their attitude based on the new information they have been confronted with, or should they maintain their previously determined modicum of thought?*

What this ultimately lends itself to is **cognitive dissonance**. This occurs when a person experiences feelings of discomfort resulting from inconsistent attitudes, thoughts, and behaviors. To avoid feelings of dissonance, people will ignore views that oppose their own, change their own beliefs to match their actions, or seek reassurances after making a difficult decision.

The common cliché has often been argued *that life isn't about finding yourself, but rather creating yourself.* I certainly recognize the merit of this cliché in the sense that each day provides a new opportunity to become something different or shape yourself into the person you hope to be. However, I still challenge the notion that life is about finding yourself. Where are you going to find that person? Who is that person if, after twenty-eight years, we still haven't met? Simply because I may not be comfortable with exactly where I am or what I am doing, does that make me any less of a person? Does that mean I still need to find myself? Perhaps the cognitive dissonance experienced by events in life, decisions, people, and influences may be responsible for shaping our lives in several ways, but that doesn't alter the reality that I found myself long ago. The argument here thus being that we aren't going through life finding ourselves, we are only becoming better or worse versions of ourselves depending on what we do and how we go about doing it. What values do we hold? What accounts for the decisions we make? Whom do we associate with? Where do we place personal successes, passions, and goals?

Recently, during a discussion of literature with a close friend about everything ranging from Ayn Rand to Stephen King, the theme of

**self-authenticity** made its way to the forefront of our conversation. We were debating the societal norms being challenged by various authors and that the lead characters in their books were always placed in roles that involved life-altering decisions and the choice of whether or not they would remain true to themselves or if the courses they charted would be dictated by the desires and pressures of others. What we found repeated through this theme was that no matter how hard these characters wrestled with the ability to stay true to themselves and to choose the uncharted path or to make the unpopular decision, they ultimately ended up in triumph through their hardships because they never fully lost their sense of self. Their strength was apparent in that they never fully succumbed to the weight of cognitive dissonance. They never truly gave up on their own sense of self. These characters were not searching to become something or someone; as my friend conveyed, these characters already knew who that someone was and realized that up until a certain point in their lives they had denied, hidden, or neglected that person. They had appeared to give up on the "authentic self." In that regard, we concluded that *we aren't living trying to find ourselves, we are living trying to be ourselves in the most genuine capacity possible.*

As our discussion furthered and I tried to build the case for living knowing my identity is found in Christ and that I already know who I am, I was countered by his rebuttal that even though I may believe those things, I am not living a life authentic to me. He verified my intelligence, work ethic, and ability to be successful no matter where I place those efforts, but he questioned my abilities to place them correctly. Or in the very least, "correctly" in the sense of being true to myself. From my perspective, I was humbled by his accolades and belief in me, but also made out to be somewhat of a hypocrite. In reflecting on my current state of life, I realized that I don't know if giving things all I have is actually creating opportunities or pulling me away from ones I could have. Yet, despite that, it's still in my nature to give my best no matter what the cause. As J.D. Salinger alludes in *Catcher in the Rye*, sometimes you still have to "play the game of life according to the rules" in order to get by. But does anyone really just want to "get by?" It sounds heartless and self-sabotaging to hold that view. However, that is exactly what I am doing right now, and it's slowly breaking me despite my efforts to hold onto who I am.

Analogically, the notion of self-authenticity and life is a lot like writing. For me, I may not know where I am going when writing, but I know what I want to say and I like the process—every single part of it. Sure it can be tedious and exhaustive, but it's in the hours of creation that the rewards are sown, whether they ever physically come to a known publishable fruition or not. And that's precisely the point—the work is valuable regardless of outcome.

One of the most infamous street skaters, Rodney Mullen, captures this concept best as he expanded on his distaste for how avarice has altered skating. "Don't frickin' skate in front of the camera, don't practice in front of the camera, don't friggin' publish it on YouTube every time you get a new trick—it's not about that," he said as he gazed at the setting sun through wraparound shades. "If you do it for the sake of loving it, and you don't care whether you're seen or not, or paid or not, all that stuff will come. But enjoy the process! If you start doing things for the sake of selling up front, for rewards, then it's going to catch up to you. The other guys not chasing money are going to outdo you in the end, because real innovation and grit come from loving the process."

I believe this is a quote worth referencing often as a reminder of why you care in the first place. It is not about the paycheck; it is about the perseverance and passion. It is not about the blue, first-place ribbon at the end of the race. I respect this idea deeply, even though sometimes it is hard to see success on a scale that isn't tainted by a world obsessed with the idea of wealth as a mandate for achievement or good fortune.

Doing something for the sake of simply loving it should be enough merit alone. Similar to musician Bob Dylan, for example, in his quest for creation over fame, in his desire to speak what needed to be said—it was that attitude and approach that ultimately saved him and his career. It wasn't the chasing of success. All of that came to him in his own living in the risk of self-authenticity. And I believe that is what we all should be doing but are too afraid to for the potential risk it brings. I, for one, am afraid of my own shadow of failure when truly, if I ever get out from behind that shadow of pseudo-safety, I might actually have a fighting chance to be authentically me. The innate fear to take a greater chance on myself is what leaves me caught living a life I feel is not, has not been, and never will be my own should I decide to perpetuate denying self in the process of creating life.

*"Therefore, I urge you, brothers and sisters, in view of God's mercy, to offer your bodies as a living sacrifice, holy and pleasing to God—this is your true and proper worship. Do not conform to the pattern of this world, but be transformed by the renewing of your mind. Then you will be able to test and approve what God's will is—his good, pleasing, and perfect will."*

Romans 12:1-2

# PART III: RACING TOWARDS CHRIST

## ONE FOOT IN FRONT OF THE OTHER

*Trusting He Will Carry You*

As I continue my quest to find the finish line, I must project well-deserved credit and accolades to the Bob Dylan-loving, supportive individual who has stood by my side, encouraged me when I needed it most, willed my tears away, and taught me that to quit is one thing, but to shrug is quite another. And to shrug without hesitation and with utmost confidence can be the most empowering and liberating thing a person can learn to do.

The time was not then, the time is not when, the time is now—the time is always now. The only time we ever truly have to manage is the present moment—it is the living of our lives embracing the moments we are given. There won't always be another time and we can't get time back that has already passed, so it is imperative to make the most of what is right here and right now.

Six months after I began my first full-time job out of college and postgraduate schooling, I decided the career choice was not right for me. The stress, the lifestyle, everything that accompanied it was never what I wanted to go after in life. But I did it because it was the safe thing; it was secure; because jobs in journalism were not panning out as I had expected and part-time work in writing was getting exhausting. And fitness jobs were fulfilling, but I didn't know how to make a career out of such a newfound passion of mine. Yet at the same time I was distraught by this venture towards a new avenue in life, a rather wise person asked me, "If you wake up thirty years from now doing what you're doing right now, will you be happy with your life? If yes, keep at it. If no, then what are you waiting for?"

So I shrugged the job as a high school English teacher in a private suburban school. I shrugged the monotony. I shrugged the schooling and training and skills I had developed and I said I can't do this anymore. I cried and wrestled with endless doubts and suffocating fears, but I had the courage to move on and to move forward with God's plan for my life. He never promised the race would be easy. And He never promised a lack of detours, but He did gift us with HIS promise that HIS will shall be done and we are guaranteed heaven and eternal life through Him. That is life that matters. That is life worth living. That is the NOW we all need to know and engage within. The perspective we need to see is God's—not ours. Ours is meaningless in comparison.

However, ask anyone close to me and they'll tell you that getting there hasn't been easy for me. On a bitterly cold January 2nd, just weeks after my resignation and merely one day into a New Year, which should have been filled with hope, expectation, and new opportunity, my attitude conveyed in my journal read something like this:

*It's a New Year, but I feel old with each hour that passes. A new grind is setting in, but my head isn't in any game and my feet aren't training for any race. What am I waiting for and what am I doing? Today, I taught a bootcamp fitness class and you know what? It was awesome. My energy was fresh, people were sweating and smiling, but afterwards I felt empty and hollow. I walked into the locker room and shamed myself for my own body image. Since battling an eating disorder in high school and college, I've been so far past that—so far removed from the shame of a mirror or scale, but it taunted me again today. I felt that grip of self-loathing, imperfection, and hatred. Nothing good ever comes of that. I looked into a mirror instead of up at God, where my redemptive reflection needs to be found. I want to feel whole again. I want to feel worthy. I am wanted by an amazing man. But how do I even deserve his love? Me?! In quitting my job I feel empty, but relieved. The agony of one pain is gone, but the agony of uncertainty is perhaps much worse. I know God is working, but I don't see how and I can't discern why. Time is slipping through my fingers at a pace I can't control. I feel lost and afraid. It is as though I am alone in space with a destiny forgotten.*

Later that same week in January, I hadn't yet found answers, but after a great deal of prayer, I wrote the following:

*If there's tragedy in the mystery, I've yet to discover it. If there's light in the darkness, I'm yet to see it. If madness drives success, I'll be one to experience it. But if tolerance for all drives anger and fuels listlessness, I'll have unmitigated passion the rest of life. So set goals. See God. Reach. Do. Be! Just be.*

We live in a culture of competition. An arena where we shift and we measure, we compare and we catalog, we share and we enlist. We strive without stopping, and we mount worthiness and accomplishments as needing to be saddled with money and achievements. Is this wealth? Is that success? The simple conclusion is that there will always be endless emptiness with that perception.

However, if we harness the ability to hone our skills and see every activity as worthwhile—whether for pleasure or productivity, we can move forward with the right mindset.

God created us to be thinkers, problem-solvers, and innovators. He gave us this world to use! But first and foremost, he wants for us to spread his love and his message no matter what we are doing. Whether that's being unemployed and discovering new ways to serve with our talents and passions or if we are toiling endlessly, let us find glory in Him and in the present moment of NOW. Remember: there's then, there's when, and there's now. Make the time count.

So what if maybe I am on the sidelines tying my shoes, or maybe my legs are too tired to keep going, or maybe my heart aches from the weight of personal failure? Because, here's the thing: no matter how many difficult, doubt-filled days come my way, I'll still lace up those shoes, mend my heart, reach out for help, kneel to pray, and I'll get back in the race. And it is not the race for everything under the sun, but it is the race for life through Christ. And that's the only race worth running. It is the race that beckons us all towards the eternal finish line of love, hope, and enduring promise in HIM.

*"Blessed is the man who remains steadfast under trial, for when he has stood the test he will receive the crown of life, which God has promised to those who love him."*

James 1:12

# PRESS ONWARD

*Knowing the Prize Is Worth Attaining*

Caged within the Complacent Carousel of Life: if you're only seeking the finish line, you will find no purpose in the journey of life.

The Shamrock Shuffle is here! And guess what?! It's going to be a "Shamrocking awesome" good time! The Shamrock Shuffle is a popular, annual 8K race that I love to run as an exciting way to kick off racing season in Chicago, Illinois. It marks a notable transition to spring and, overall, an exciting time of year. As the first race of the season, my training for it is nothing dramatic or even admirable, but I work towards a decent pace to loosen up my legs and to have that feeling of getting back in the game for the summer racing season ahead.

It's a race that beckons my participation and success normally without any hint of dissatisfaction. However, I distinctly remember one Shamrock Shuffle I ran, and instead of racing for a personal record, I decided that because I was experiencing a breakup at the time and other family struggles, I would just run the race and do my best to enjoy myself. I lacked my usual moxie and enthusiasm, but still had every intent to finish the race and to finish it strong. Standing within the starting corral, amassed by thousands of other runners struggling to keep their body temperatures normalized on a brisk, yet sunny April morning, I set my purple Garmin watch for time and pace, selected my iTunes playlist, said a seemingly rehearsed prerace prayer and tried to get in the racing zone. But for some reason, I could not get into that zone or clear my mind. I was shivering cold, distracted, and questioning everything. I was unable to focus on the race and I begrudgingly kept thinking to myself *how soon until this one's over?*

Shrugging off my attitude but trapped in the marplot of my own thoughts for another half hour waiting to begin the race, I realized I was at a place in life where I was living but I wasn't really living. I was going through the motions, the days, the work, the stress, the ups, the downs, the seeking of discernment, but I wasn't living. The type of living where you can actually taste your food, experience those moments of overwhelming laughter, the times where you want to run until your legs might give way, when embracing the sight of a smile that lights up your day and the beauty of allowing love to fully harness every corner of your heart is profoundly moving. That was the living I craved, and the living I had lost.

As the starting shot blared, soaring into the vast, blue, skyscraper-lined city sky, I wasn't at all excited to run. I had barely even allowed myself to hear the gunshot. *Did the race just start?* I wondered. *Wait? What race is this? Where am I? How far do I have to run? Maybe I'll give in and walk part of it. No, no I can't do that....*

The herd of runners started moving and I followed suit as though to embody mimicry and nothing else. My toes were numb from the cold, and my mind was locked from wrestling with the reality that I had no desire to be there in that race at that time and on that day. The moment was fleeting, but I kept my feet moving. I turned on my music, hit the start button on my watch, but my thoughts weren't on any finish line. They were—surprisingly—on the journey. As I ran along at a painfully slow pace for myself, the brutal cold snapped at my face, and my toes and eyes tingled from a constant blustery chill. With each step forward on the blackened pavement I felt movement of my body, but no physical effort to rightfully support it. There was movement without momentum, thoughts without distinction. I was running, yes—racing, no. People were casually passing me on my right and left, the job that I normally reserved for myself to do to others, but during this race I had found a stride that I didn't want to alter. In ways, it somewhat felt to me like a pity run. Why did I spend money to race and then just come jog for kicks? I wasn't motivated to work harder, nor was I opposed to running slower. A long time ago I learned that you can't expect to win every race you run, but you can and still should expect to challenge yourself personally each and every time.

So, there I was alongside 30,000 other people out for themselves and I refused to race them and refused to race against myself. I was fighting the passion for purpose as it was swallowed up by the coils of complacency. My body was icy to the touch, but numb for reasons beyond the brace of external temperatures. As I continued my modified stride, passing red flashing mile-markers with no regard for the time listed or my mile long splits, I was temporarily aware and consumed by the notion that I had become comfortable with complacency. It was a striving to *not* care to strive. A will to allow myself to not need that "will." In a way it was liberating, but in another way, paralyzing. It was saying, *Good for you*, but *Don't be getting better at anything fast, No need to try.*

Intrigued by the commonality of my complacent thoughts, I slowed my pace more, even as my body lurched forward towards the sights and sounds I readily ignored during any typical race. There were encouraging disc jockeys lining the streets providing soundtracks to elevate the mood and energy of the runners, there were fans up and down the streets waving clever signs and holding obnoxious cowbells, and there were children on tall shoulders who idolized each runner as a rock star.

I noticed neon tape on the ground guiding my path, smiles from a volunteer, an exquisite skyline backdrop that captivated runners as we weaved through the city streets. The damp smell of a dew carpeted early spring morning mixed with gasoline pooled on dirty streets, and random food trucks mellowing out the atmosphere with the sweet warmth of pastry-rising temptation. I took notice of the world around me and observed without guilt. I almost gave in to walk a few steps so I could feel as though I had the ability to slow down the fleeting passage of time. Then slowly, unexpectedly—and something runners in the middle of a bitter cold race rarely do—I grinned from ear to ear. I had briefly forgotten who I was, where I was, and even why I was what I was. But the rest of the world was carrying that torch for a moment and I wasn't accountable for being the do-er. I didn't have the obligation to be the sprinter, the leader, or the winner. It wasn't wrong to feel this sense of relief for that particular time and space of yet another race, but within me, the fear of the permanence of passivity wasn't altogether "right" to feel either.

Nonetheless, after I passed the final mile marker, heard the echoed clamor of cowbells and whistles, and caroused onward knowing the finish line was near, I set my heart in motion, my legs back in gear, uncovered my face from the cozy warmth of a festive green-and-white shamrock-patterned windsock encircling my neck, and propelled my mind and body towards the finish. I had reserved energy the entire race and though I felt tired, my adrenaline got a hold of me. When I could finally see that finish line around the last turn, I broke from the ambling herd of runners and sprinted all the way through the finish until I heard my personalized finisher confirmation, "Andrea Cladis! Number 3178" resonate over the loud speakers.

Once my legs slowed their pace after making it through the finish with a forceful spring and recoil, that infamous post-run flush and swell whelmed my body and somehow I felt both relief and sorrow. Relief that I still had that sprint left in me, but sorrow that the race was over, sorrow there were no more sights to see or people to experience, or moments to put on a slow-tracked pause. Minutes passed and I was distracted gazing around at the spectators, simply taking in the experience; I realized I never even looked at the clock when I finished. I had hardly glanced at my watch. I had no idea how long the race took me to complete, nor did I even care. It wasn't important. What I did need, though, was to be reminded that there is a finish line in every race and eventually you will get there whether you want to or not. That same finish line exists in life, too, so bumbling along with no direction and no sense of urgency or care won't stop time or delay the inevitable. We have to run our race and know that it won't always be a perfect day. And no, we are not crazy dare-we-choose-to-cruise when our legs refuse to run at an unsustainable pace. Even so, the lesson we still learn is that we can't concede either.

So, addlepated as I was, I realized that no matter what the race, I am always finding the finish line because that is the place where personal victory is the most rewarding, and the place where we are gratified by the unexpected tenacity of our own will and indomitable strength.

I am not advocating that you will the finish line away, but don't ignore it either. In your complacency take time to revel in life, but get back on course, chase after what you want, dare to be the best possible version of "you" that you can be, and don't huddle in the herd for too long.

Dissipate discernment.

Challenge complacency.

Remember the FINISH—because it can wait, but it won't.

Above all else, even if you're jogging, keep running! It's when you stop altogether that your limbs freeze, your mind becomes restless, your body becomes numb, and you lose your will to press on. Never neglect time, however, to slow down and admire the scenery along the way. Remember to keep moving and to keep running your race, because that finish line will greet you just around the corner long before you'll ever feel prepared to welcome its arrival.

"No, in all these things we are more than conquerors through him who loved us. For I am convinced that neither death nor life, neither angels nor demons, neither the present nor the future, nor any powers, neither height nor depth, nor anything else is all creation, will be able to separate us from the love of god that is in Christ Jesus our Lord."

Romans 8:37–39

~~~~~~~~~~~~~~~~~~~~~~~~~~~~~~~~~~~~~~~~~~~

# ENDURANCE MATTTERS
*Assuring Provision through Mercy*

*No discipline seems pleasant at the time, but painful. Later on, however, it produces a harvest of righteousness and peace for those who have been trained by it.*

*Hebrews 12.11*

One of the most difficult races I ever finished was during the hot July summer of 2015 in Indianapolis, Indiana. The race itself was a longer sprint distance triathlon which was part of the TRI Indy series of summer races. When I registered for this particular race several months prior, my rationale was that the location was near my brother's home in Indiana, and the race fell on his birthday and anniversary weekend. I presumed that if I planned to compete in a race that weekend, it would essentially accomplish two goals: one, it would force my family to travel to visit my brother and his wife, while also welcoming my brother's involvement in a passion of mine; and two, the more selfish reason – I knew that the provision of a rare allowance of a midsummer trip would be a worthwhile venture for both my busy, monotonous schedule and addlepated mind.

As the second official triathlon I was to compete in that summer, I was already well into my training season heading into the race; however, I had not adequately balanced my training plan with healthy eating, the volume of fitness classes I teach, and the normal race training schedule I was accustomed to following. Though I had been eagerly anticipating the race, during the last two weeks leading up to race day, I hit a training rut and a low I had never experienced before when preparing for a triathlon. I recall feeling weak, sluggish, and lethargic in every way. My usual race taper was not effectively topping off my dwindling training efforts and, as a result, I was past anxious about both my physical and mental condition heading into the race.

Lacking confidence to the point of not even wanting to compete in the race at all, race day came upon me faster than expected and soon I was reluctantly packing my bright orange triathlon bag with race-day gear—from swimsuits, goggles, bike shorts, towels, a bike helmet and biking gloves to shoes, extra socks, a wetsuit, snacks, and all the necessary items I would need to compete. Normally I am so nervous before a race that I select my race-day clothing and lay it out at least a week before race day, but between my beleaguered physical and mental state, I felt I would be lucky if in the very least I did not forget to pack anything. Nonetheless, I stuffed in the last few extra towels, zipped up my orange bag, completed one last tune-up on my bike, and successfully but slowly completed a final evening prerace swim the night before my family was planning to leave for Lafayette, IN, the town where my brother lives. With a deep pit of despair in my stomach, I fell asleep that night knowing that less than 48 hours now remained until the race.

The following morning after loading the car with my bike and gear, my parents and I drove through the ever exciting Indiana countryside towards Lafayette, where we were planning to go out to eat in celebration of my brother's birthday and then drive the early morning trek to Indy from his home for the race the following morning. As endless farmland, prairie, and wind turbines flooded my glazed vision as I stared out the window on that cloudy morning, I was consumed by unrelenting doubt and regret. Doubt in myself and my abilities, and regret that I thought this entire venture with my family in tow was a good idea. The reality that my entire family was going to be there to cheer me on and I had lost any and all thrill towards the reality of the race I was to participate in, more than ever I feared letting them down and being a disappointment. My thoughts spiraled down a chamber of self-deprecation and my physical state of lethargy and continued stomach discomfort, a result of IBS-induced stress and anxiety, left me feeling depressed and abysmally dreading what was to come.

As the clouds coalesced to bring in an afternoon cold front of windy storms to the city of Lafayette, we finally made it through increasingly forceful rains to a quaint restaurant where my brother and his wife awaited our arrival and his official birthday dinner celebration. Though I was grateful to spend time with my family, in self-absorbed vanity, I was more concerned about what I would eat for dinner because not only do I have digestive problems, but for years I also have always eaten the same prerace meal consisting of a light or gluten-free pasta, fresh, herbed tomato sauce, a plain lettuce salad, a small serving of steamed broccoli, two slices of bread (without the crusts because superstition sometimes gets the best of athletes, myself included), and a tall glass of chocolate almond milk.

Now in my third year of triathlon racing, I had never eaten anything different as my last meal before a race, but instead of trying to allay food fears in a rational way and feeling afraid to eat much from the restaurant menu, I drank some of my mom's diet Coke, scarfed far too much bread from the restaurant (with crusts intact; no, not that that matters...) alongside homemade nut butters I brought with me in hopes that at least the carbs and protein would sustain me through the morning race. Soon, however, I would learn that this combination was perhaps one of the worst things I could have done to myself and my nerves on the eve of a big race.

Overly focused on my unusually heightened nerves for the TRI Indy race, I struggled to give my brother the attention he deserved during dinner to properly celebrate *his* birthday and *his* anniversary. I was antsy, agitated, and kept having to leave the table for the bathroom throughout our dinner meal. My parents found my actions incredibly rude, and while they understood my anxiety, they did not have patience for my inability to set aside worry and enjoy the evening.

That night after we unpacked at my brother's home and I once again compulsively organized my race gear, I hardly spoke with my parents, and after everyone went to bed, I was unable to fall asleep. I called a friend in the middle of the night looking for guidance, solace, and assurance to build up my confidence, but unfortunately that was not to be found.

So there I sat at three in the morning on the newly carpeted floor of my brother's spacious living room, listening to the quiet rain, sobbing for feelings of imminent failure before I had even started something, and for the same pensive doubts and regrets that plagued me on the drive from Chicago to Lafayette.

Trying to dissolve my tears in my loose jersey nightshirt, I browsed their bookshelf where I noticed several familiar Christian titles. As I prayed a broken prayer into my tear-stained nightshirt, I was gently reminded that I was surrounded by a family who rests their hope in Christ and not on the sole merit of accomplishments such as being a champion of a local triathlon. I began to realize the foolishness of my worry and the futility of continued self-defeating thoughts. While prayer was not coming easily, I worked to shift my focus from the race itself to Christ and how he would help me through it regardless of whether my performance reflected the state of my weary body or now rumbling stomach full of gluten-heavy restaurant bread, an excessive consumption of nut butters, and dehydrating soda.

After reading a few short passages from random books I snagged from their shelves, I was finally able to settle down and embrace sleep, if only for a few hours. My typical race-day nerves woke me up promptly at 4:45 AM to drive into Indianapolis with my father as the rest of my family—mom, brother, and sister—planned to sleep in and come closer to race time where despite my shallow attitude the day prior, they would serve as supportive spectators of my race-day efforts.

As my dad and I drove together to Indy, we silently took in the post-rain soaked morning sunrise and briefly discussed the race ahead. Still, in an ever thoughtful state, I thanked God for how blessed I was for the many times my father spent with me driving to early morning runs, triathlons, and other athletic events, wherein his presence and coaching meant everything to me. And yet again, even after the long drive to my brother's house the day prior, my dad gladly, selflessly, and with a desire in his heart to always be there for me, led us on the journey to Indianapolis.

Our conversation danced from topic to topic, which was a needed and welcomed distraction for me until I dozed off for a short time along the drive. My father kindly woke me as we arrived and in our usual fashion, investigated the race site—a breathtaking, wooded, hilly park in the largest recreation area in Indianapolis.

We both agreed that the scenery was stunningly exquisite for a race! I would get to take in a beautiful open-water swim in a clear, cold water lake, the rolling, forested hills on a crisp summer morning appeared to be most suitable terrain for the partial open road bike ride, and the innumerous wooded trails beckoned my enthusiasm for the final running leg of the race.

As I commenced the race in my age group category, my stomach was churning. I felt bloated, uncomfortable, and felt pain locking up the cadence of breathing in my chest. It was a strange combination of IBS pain, allergies, asthma, and injuries from progressive training and a failed taper. I made the decision not to wear my wetsuit, and that was probably my first mistake of the race. The water looked gorgeous, reflecting the morning sunlight, but deceptively turned out to be awfully frigid. Upon my running entrance to start the swim, I immediately began hyperventilating and could not catch my breath. Normally my strongest and fastest leg of the race, I was panicking, paddling in the water, trying to warm up my body, while swallowing copious amounts water and struggling to breathe. Flailing in distress, I closed my eyes and put my head down to swim. After only two full freestyle strokes I had to surface again, and this time gasping for air more than before. I flipped over on my back to open up my chest cavity and lungs, but it only made me cough more. I saw the buoy markers and boats in the water where rescue men waited in case someone needed help in the water or to be removed from the race. Those men and women I have hardly noticed in any other race looked friendly and kind to me today. Calmed by their presence I could see out of the corner of my eye, I kept paddling through the water, unable to really swim, all while getting pushed and shoved at all sides not knowing if this would be the first race I voluntarily forfeited on the first leg. But sometimes in life despite discomfort, a lack of oxygen, and mounting fear, you have to put your head down and keep swimming. And that's exactly what I did. Toes frozen, lungs contracting, and an unforgiving deep lake to conquer, I swam the best I could. I rotated between freestyle strokes and backstroke to pace out my breathing with the goal of continued progress through the water. It was motivation, determination, will, and my feisty spirit that surfaced again in those cold waters, and I knew that no matter the challenge I would get through the race.

When the shore was finally in sight, the water was shallow enough to put my feet down to touch the sandy bottom of the lake and I started propelling myself off the bottom towards the shore. Water-logged, freezing, and out of breath, I was hardly able to run to the transition area, but seeing my dad not far from the bike zone, I felt relief and the look in his face told me he knew something was wrong. Flustered, I got back into my groove, found my orange bag and race station among the many others in the transition area, and got ready for the biking leg of the race. Toweled off, check, shoes on, check, helmet, check, sunglasses, check... I went through the motions with more difficulty than usual, but finally I was off towards the bike mounting area and onto the bike leg of the race where my dad yelled at me to get my butt moving and race! I smiled at his sarcasm still chilled from the swim, and I pushed hard into the first hill, though still failing to get a deep breath. I knew that all I had to do now was just keep pedaling, another 16 miles, and my family would be there to get me through the last running leg of the race.

Those 16 miles were far from pleasant, but I cycled as I have never cycled before. Gasping for breath the entire time, overly exhausted from the swim, my fears resurfaced on that leg of the race as I felt weaker than ever on some of the steep, hilly climbs of the course. I can hardly recall the scenery I so desperately wanted to take in, but I do remember pedaling hard, closing my eyes, and putting my head down to cycle just as I had during the swim.

When I finally dismounted my bike back in the transition zone and torpidly took off for the last running leg of the race, I knew that 'one foot in front of the other,' I was going to do it and I was going to finish. My stomach was aggravating me past my breaking point, though, and about half a mile into the run, I stopped to use a bathroom along the course. Again this is something I had never done before during a race because I am always competing against myself and others to achieve the fastest race time and hopefully to place in my age group. Tossing all those hopes aside, my goal remained to finish. And *that* I was going to do. Four miles, three miles, two miles, one mile ... I counted down as debilitating tingling flooded my calves and quads, and with each stride I felt as though a backpack of bricks was saddled on my back. S-curved sweat formed and slid down my face, chest, arms, and legs; I talked myself out of my own head and kept a prayerful attitude. Seeking out a few fellow athletes ahead of me to motivate my speed on the last part of the run, I blocked out the pain, continued taking fast, shallow breaths, and let sweat blur my vision as I came to the hardest, yet most rewarding part of any race I have ever completed. The final 400 to the finish. As with all races, my spunk surfaces near the end and I spotted my final targets.

This time, I picked out the two male athletes not too far ahead of me that I was determined to defeat.

Forcing my way through the final 400 meters of the race, I took off into a sprint, feeling like I might go to the bathroom while running, struggling to breathe, and experiencing muscle cramping from head to toe, I tore past those two dudes in my way and smeared through the finish line. And trust me in this: I had never been happier in my life to see the finish line than I was for that race! My family swelling the finish area with their presence smiled and cheered obnoxiously when I crossed the finish line. I felt miserable and performed terribly, but wanted to show strength in the finish, especially for my brother, who had never been to one of my triathlons before. Their joyfulness, teasing words, and victorious shouts were heartwarming to me as I slowed my run and took off towards the bathroom. I was sweating in agony, and glad the race was over.

Sitting in an overused port-o-john, perspiring profusely, loathing taking on the post-race flush in addition to feeling sick, salty sweat mixed with tears as I bemoaned my state of being. I was stuck not only in the most disgusting type of bathroom, but in the position of wanting to show gratitude and be energetic, all smiles for my family, but physically wanting a cool shower, cleared lungs, and rest.

Nonetheless, when I walked out of that bathroom and stumbled towards my bike to gather my orange bag and race gear from its station in the transition zone, I saw my family all together, smiling, chatting, and enjoying the warmth and blessing of God's creations on a beautiful summer Sunday morning.

As disappointed as I was in my personal race results, I knew in that instant that all I had wanted had been achieved in that very moment. The race wasn't about me or my stomach or my training or my pain. The race was not even about experiencing a gorgeous, Indiana destination. The "race" was about moving closer to Christ—as a family, celebrating a birthday, momentarily smiling, and prayerfully giving praise to God for his eternal blessings on our lives.

"You finished the race, Trice!" my brother gibed while drinking my post-race chocolate milk knowing I was less than happy with my performance. "But what was up with all those dudes in spandex?! Oh, my goodness! These 'triathlon' people. It's weird."

Heartened by his continued commentary and observational critiques, my stomach pain failed to dissipate as I worked to gather my racing items. Sweat trickled down the small of my mud-splattered back, an unforgiving sunburn began to reveal its malevolent glow atop my shoulders. Yet, amidst my physical discomfort, I was whelmed once again by the deeper meaning of this race. And that meaning stood in the shade of towering oak trees about 25 yards outside of the transition area where triathletes of all ages were refueling, confabulating, and cleaning up in the post-race hustle. As I fumbled with my empty water bottle, mess of towels, shoes, headbands, and wetsuit, I gleaned happily at the nexus that was my family.

I saw my strong mother, the breast cancer survivor with a newly replaced left knee, the selfless family caretaker, and cheerleader for that which brings her most joy and pride in life—her children.

I glanced at my wise father, the coach, baseball fanatic, and gentleman aging with grace; a man whose life work has been as a physician with hands of healing for the Lord.

My sturdy brother, who has grown into a man of unrelenting faith, a supportive husband and church leader, but someone who fights personal demons that impact his daily ability to feel fulfillment in life.

My angelic sister, my very best friend, whose ever-ready smile, genuine compassion, and heart of purity has been the sparkle that has uplifted our family unit in all times of hardship or tragedy.

Looking upon my family in a way that made me feel closer to Christ and the heaven He provides for us here on earth, the speed of my compulsive fidgeting and obsessive organization of my items slowed as I studied my family members gently listening to shared stories, smiling, carousing in the warm breeze and shadows of perfection in a summer day.

*That is my family. That is my team!* I thought. *That is where my hope rests in the safety of our dysfunction, but ever-enduring trust and belief in God.*

As I walked over to join my family team, we laughed, we teased, we smiled, we later enjoyed a delicious brunch together, and the triathlon I had feared so much quickly became the backdrop of a weekend racing for faith, family, and the assurance of mercy in Christ.

Sitting quietly at brunch was when I fully realized the rarity of having my entire family together once again, and I was soon enveloped with joy for the moment, peace in the race, and solitude in the stillness of my desire to remain whole in Christ's provision for my life.

Closeness to Christ is not designed to be a solitary journey or lonely pursuit. God calls us to fellowship in Him, and when we gather together in His name, it is right there with us that He will be.

*"Fight the good fight of the faith. Take hold of the eternal life to which you were called when you made your good confession in the presence of many witnesses."*

1 Timothy 6:12

# FALL ON YOUR FAITH

*Your legs will never falter if their strength is derived through grace*

Endurance through trials is what builds our faith; trusting in Christ's purpose is what sustains our hope.

I spend a lot of time observing people around me—listening, watching, waiting, and desiring to know what their stories are and how those stories have shaped their lives. I want to know because I am curious, because I care, and because I am genuinely fascinated by the wisdom I gain through knowledge of experiences or choices made by those around me. I crave answers where there is mystery and guidance where I witness undeniable faith.

Recently, while listening to a conversation between an engaged couple discussing future plans, I heard a phrase that has become cliché through television, movies, or other shallow, mediated perceptions of relational distress. As the woman I was observing leaned across the table over her untouched coffee and yogurt parfait to whisper something to the man/her fiancé sitting across from her, she unexpectedly removed the beautifully polished engagement ring from her finger, placed it on the table, sat back, and casually said, "It's not you, hun, it's me. I can't do this anymore. I just can't. And I won't." Chapfallen, I watched as the man, refusing to continue to fight for her love, fell to defeat, lost faith in what he once had, held out his hands and asked in one final effort, "What have I done to lose your love? Why am I not the man for you?" While I felt discouragement trample my insides and felt the weight of despair the man stood to endure, I wondered what would have made this woman let go of the faith I presume this couple once shared. What was it that made her say, "I don't have faith in you. I don't have faith in us"? Of course there could be hundreds of reasons that I am unaware of for why this couple was no longer able to move forward or perhaps why there was a loss of faith in a love that I know had at least a five-year history. Yet, regardless of the reasoning or explanation to be given, the albatross we all bear is that we're human. We. Are. Human. We have emotions and feelings. We make mistakes. We judge. We criticize. We place unrealistic expectations on ourselves and others. We fail in patience. We lack in forgiveness. We are innately weak. And we rarely choose to love like Christ.

Evidently, relationships aren't perfect and maybe in the case of this particular couple, separating was the right decision for them, but it forces me to pose the enduring question again: "Why faith?" And not just faith in others but, specifically, why faith *in Christ*?

Why? Because HIS love is a PERFECT love. In the context of witnessing such a heartbreaking situation it becomes clear why, as followers of Christ, we must have faith. Humans are inherently flawed; we are imperfect beings, and we can't always see past imperfections in others. We can't always trust those around us because they will betray us, they will abandon us, and they will reject us without reason. God's promise is different, though. His promise is everlasting. His desire to be with us never ceases. His love for us will not ever end. His mercy is too great. His grace is far more than what we deserve, but it's given freely. We can have unabashed faith because we know these things. We know He will never leave, He will never cast us aside, and He will never run, even if and when we stray. This is a promise that should give us incontrovertible purpose. It should provide us with an undercurrent of hopeful gratitude in our lives. It should allow us to garner our strength, hone our resolve, and give direction to desires of our heart.

Faith isn't the result of simply "acting" righteous or the perception of being so. Faith isn't good deeds or being a "good" person. We are often tempted to do the right thing for the wrong reason because we think we will be rewarded for our righteousness, but righteousness for the sake of a facade or for an earthly reward will never bring us satisfaction. Genuine righteousness is what counts, meaning that it is not what we do, but why we do it. What is the motivation in our hearts? The book of Psalms reminds us that the more you're in God's word, the more you'll love his commandments and want to pursue righteousness out of a love for him. Therefore, righteousness, even in terms of faith, isn't putting "God on a shelf" in your life and only seeking his mercy or grace in times of need.

Faith is not the struggle or the hardship, but rather it is the result of endurance through trials, hope in Christ, trust in His will, and a consistent desire to grow closer to Him in every possible way, every single day.

Faith is the bond between Christ and His followers; it is what allows for complete trust in the unknown. Faith is the unshakeable foundation we must build in Christ, through Christ, and for Christ.

Without faith, we can't possibly have trust or belief in God, but with faith—with a steadfast desire to build that relationship with Him—we stand to inherit the ultimate gift which has been promised to us—the Kingdom of heaven.

*"Don't be afraid, I've redeemed you. I've called your name.
You're mine. When you're in over your head, I'll be there
with you. When you're in rough waters, you will not go down.
When you're between a rock and a hard place, it won't be
a dead end because I am your God. Your personal God, the
Holy Israel, your Savior. I paid a huge price for you! That's
how much you mean to me! That's how much I love you!"*

Isaiah 43:1-4

# PART IV: FACING THE FINISH

## GROWTH IN FAILURE
*Purpose, Renewal & Relationship*

*The only thing that can veritably thwart progressive growth is your opposition to success and your appeasement in failure.*

As I find myself scrambling to lesson plan, write syllabi, arrange classrooms, choreograph fitness classes, and schedule more time for prayer and sleep, I have been asking myself a host of critical questions about *purpose, renewal,* and *relationship*.

**Purpose** is what drives our daily steps and call to action.

**Renewal** is what gives us energy to re-fill our cup and keep going.

**Relationship** with Christ and others is what we build upon and grow within to make the entire journey worthwhile.

Do you ever find yourself stuck in days that never seem to want to end, but when they finally do, the only thing you crave is more time? And it just so happens that it is that very time you chose to will away! Do you ever notice that some of the best opportunities are shunned away because fear overwhelms logic and reason is mistaken by our own self-inflicted feelings of guilt? How is it that we can feel fear, see fear, know its fallacy, and still become a slave to its grip on our lives?

Why is it that often when we don't get what we want or we are not in the place we'd like to be that we succumb to the idea that because of situational duress, we can't grow regardless of where we are or what we are doing in the present moment? Even if it appears an ideal situation, we yearn for something different. We slowly become aggravated by the daily grind, the shuffle, or the life we wish was being lived more intentionally. And so in turn, we fail to realize the persistent opportunity we have for growth.

With each new day we are given a chance to learn something new! Perhaps that means we can explore a new skill, create something we never knew ourselves to be capable of, engage with someone in a new way, foster meaningful relationships, and even dare to discover love in all its facets. We can be bold and we can take risks. So, the question to ask yourself is, "Why hold back?" Why not fail forward and not ever again look backward?

Try. Fail. Risk. Explore. Grow! Because life is not to be lived in the consummation of work or the constant distractions that draw our focus in scattered directions. Life is to be lived in the margins where we find purpose. It is to be lived in those tiny spaces we carve out to experience what it means to be alive. Living is taking a breath of spontaneous laughter after a long day. It is the relational capacity we build with others through trial or hardship, the midnight dance that allays anxiety and captivates the moving emotions of our heart, the endless conversations that take us away when we still have much left to do, the humor that lightens our darkest days, the first smile of an infant encountering the world through a lens of innocence, the teammate who congratulates and affirms your winning efforts, the elderly couple still basking in the glow of youthful love, the family member who reaches out just to check in and see how you're doing, or the stranger who willingly asks another, "Are you okay?" These experiences exist within the deliberate framework of actively living through purpose, renewal, and relationship. These are the very fulcrums of life we must create and allow for without question.

Yes, the beating pulse of balancing work, life, and other commitments can create tension. Establishing purpose, finding spaces for renewal, and investing in relationship requires consistent and conscientious effort. Yet the lesson, however, is pacifying. Maturing and growing in the responsibility you have towards your passions, while acknowledging the privilege of the work that is right in front of you, provides an avenue for fulfillment of self-growth through discovering identity and enduring purpose.

As the margins of your life begin to reveal their shape, I challenge you to be thankful for where you are right now, to learn to fail forward, and to eagerly make room for those life-giving margins beyond your control. Embrace risks whenever you can, fail without fear, and harness success – even those seemingly miniscule personal achievements that only you can quietly boast about.

*"Do not lie to each other, since you have taken off your old self with its practices and have put on the new self, which is being renewed in knowledge in the image of its Creator."*

Colossians 3:9-10

~~~~~~~~~~~~~~~~~~~~~~~~~~~~~~~~~~~~~~~~~~~~

# CARRYING THE CROSS
*The Unbreakable Spirit of the Seamstress*

## Coffee's On

An empty table. A chilled, lamp-lit corner. The enviously replicated wood cabin coffee house hummed with espresso machines and the murmur of quiet conversations spurred along by random infusions of laughter or shrieks of frustrated tempers. Overzealous women accompanied by well-dressed men demanded attention be given to their expensive drinks and scones, scraggly musicians composed confused bars and medleys, contemplative writers scribbled endlessly searching for story, and an elderly seamstress, whose delicate hands matched her wardrobe which presented itself as a patchwork of her life's consternation and unmet desires, was there at that coffee house again.

She was always there. Waiting, watching, listening, and contentedly working on her next project. The colorful threads and yarns, beading and stitching, waiting patiently and watching carefully. She had a gentle soul, a soft smile, and a protective air about her being. No matter the time of day, every time I entered that worn coffee shop, she was the single fixture that never changed. Though a part of me feared speaking to her as if she was an untouchable enigma, she was so tangibly present that deep within me I wanted to know who was behind her tea-stained teeth, her long, coarse white hair, those fashionably vintage, red-framed reading glasses, and the marvel of her worn hands going about their daily work. Up and over, pulling front and back, teasing threads, dancing hands, indelible work – she craved the innocence of silent admiration. I could only stare in wonder or awe as the simplicity of her work and presence fascinated my being. She brought me peace, a sense of comfort, a promise of sameness I failed to find anywhere else in my life.

As I watched in waning wonderment I kept thinking to myself, I wish someone had told me it was *not* going to be easy. I wish someone had let go of my hand and said, "Hey this world isn't going to be so great all the time," or "Embrace failure! It will greet you a lot." I was on the verge of discovering something every adult longs to ignore, but must inhale in this life. It's the very notion that life is a wretched ride of uncertainty. We are conditioned to grow up in a way that makes us believe the chess pieces will all line up if we just roll the dice correctly or that the game board will swing in our favor if we work hard to win or that winning actually means something. It's a response bred from a young age – do good and you'll get good, or do well and you'll be great. But the actual reality of that is all a simple phony farce as *Catcher in the Rye's* Holden Caulfield might admit of "playing the game of life by the rules." Just follow the rules – follow the playbook set out before you and settle for a mediocre job and a mediocre life and an average family, and the placard of met needs and quenchable wants. It is security sold as pre-destined sanity, when the only end that's met is a drive towards insanity.

The grind, the shift, the workload, the hours of breaking down towards the hapless feeling of daily living. I had become a part of it. The mind numbing laboring and unfulfilling feeling of existing. So day after day I placed my bedraggled frame in that coffee house before my routine visit to the gym and I observed the strange characters who resided there, while monotonously sifting through stacks of ungraded papers and assessments I knew were meaningless to score. And in doing my daily penance, I became another cog in the wheel, a motion to feed the machine.

I sat there, unreservedly despondent, on one bitterly cold January evening in Chicago feeling lonely, lost, afraid, and seeking purpose without truth or the immediate need for grace. I wondered if I would always feel so alone. Maybe not just the physical loneliness, but everything that came with it. The sadness and the longing. The crying and the self-doubt. I watched in dismay as the life I knew melted from my eyes. The trembling that came in those moments when I knew the end was all but always going to be there. Only one thing is certain in this life, I thought, that *no one gets out alive*. And what must we make of that reality but to lie to ourselves that each day it gets better when each day we get closer. Closer to that very end we've always known from the beginning. Closer to the moment we know we cannot avoid. There isn't winning and there isn't losing. There is just closing in, dissolving, and ending. And surely the time the ending comes will only be at the time the beginning can freely admit that the end has a place and a purpose.

Resisting the urge to pull out my phone and drown my spiraling sorrows in the savage deception of social media posts, I saw the seamstress and her delicate hands enter my frame of view again.

Looking at me with renewed curiosity while squinting at the tarnished crucifix on my tangled necklace chain she probed gently, "What is it like to know God?" I'm quite certain I stared at her for several seconds in a trance of confusion at the sound of her voice as the sheer magnitude of the question she had just asked landed in my lap. In my childish way, I saw her as an angelic figure in that coffee house. Someone who certainly knew God and knew of His blessings. But the race of her life had taken her different places and maybe, I thought, she wanted her final laps to be discovering the God. *What is it like to know God?* I replayed the question over and over again in my head.

Stuttering in my response, I offered her a seat next to me and watched intently as yarns of every color I'd ever seen fell from her arms and she hesitantly, though with the grace of gratitude, sat down beside me. Her voice softened as she adjusted the light blue wool of her sweater until her thin collar bones were concealed once again.

"I want to know," she asked again. "I see your light. There is something in you that I want to know."

Attempting to show respect, I replied, "Well, I'm happy to talk to you about this. My name is Andrea, but you can call me Andi. How may I address you?"

"Oh, sure. Agnes or Ms. Plear. Just not Aggie, please. Thank you for being willing to talk to me. I've wanted to interrupt you for months, but you always appear so content in your work."

I watched her long, silver hair wither in its braids as I studied her. "It's no worry. No problem at all. Half the time I sit here wondering what to write about and make up worthless stories that no one wants to read."

She laughs. It's hearty and genuine and I feel relieved by her acceptance of my humor.

"Agnes," I begin. "What is it you want to know most? I mean, about God, of course."

"Andi, I sit here every day, knitting the very stories you sit here to write and I have always noticed a different demeanor, sparkle, zest, and connection to life that I have never seen in anyone else. And that's over 88 years of seeing people."

88? I was taken aback. There was no way!

"I'm flattered," I say.

"You have an aura of beauty and I think it's divine. No, no, I know that it is. Tell me what it is you feel. What you believe? What gives you that angelic peace? Others sense it, but I think I'm the only one that knows where it's coming from."

Tugging on the sleeves of my long-sleeved black fitted shirt and fidgeting with the now itchy violet scarf around my neck, I was suddenly aware of my presence in that coffee shop. I was usually the one doing the watching and somehow that made me feel invisible to others as though they could not possibly be there watching me back! Her commentary, while humbling, made me advertently self-aware of who I was, or who I may be to others in that place.

Reacting to my silence, she continued, "You know, Andi, I'm not here to worry or terrify you. I want to learn from you."

"I don't know what I can teach you. You've seen so much more of life than I have," I say.

"But you, you have felt so much more of it than I ever will. What is it like? What is it like?" She insisted on knowing this connection she felt I had to the divine. She wanted it to be a palpable reality, but I knew not where to begin. She weaved cautiously as I tried to formulate words.

"It's, it's, it is comfort. It is the ultimate sense of security. It is the feeling of always having purpose in all things you do – whether it is simply folding laundry or eagerly accepting a new job. It is having purpose and a willing heart even when the world strangles it."

She sorted her piles of yarn that seemed to be expanding as sincere trepidation crossed her face. "I'm not sure I understand. Why does it make you happy? What brings you that constancy of peace?"

As I looked at Agnes, not Aggie, which I desperately wanted to call her though I am not sure why, going about her work right in front of me, I knew God surely was working in her life and always had been. Through her hands, her heart, her smiles, He was present whether she knew it or not. It was then in that moment I realized that despite my prior wallowing in loneliness and despair, God was right there and He was using me as an instrument of His purpose. It was as though the race I was on had taken an about face and I was being confronted with finish line that she was weaving day after day. God was speaking and I was listening. My heart was open to His word and to her yearning.

"I am happy because I am unconditionally loved by a Father who created me perfectly. I am assured in knowing of His sacrifice for me and for you. His sacrifice for the entire world. Peace I do not always feel, but I can assure you it can only be achieved through knowing the mercy He provides."

"I am not ignorant, but I don't fully understand what you mean. Do you think I still have time to meet Him? Does He want to know me?" She wondered aloud and I felt a tinge of discouragement building in her voice.

She released her hands from the ever-ready grip of her long-knitting needles and placed them on the table as she lowered her head, letting her silver braids fall to past her shoulders. Tenderly making contact with her right hand by placing my fingertips near hers on the table, I looked into her tamed, gray eyes, "He already does," I said. "And you already do."

A single tear found its way to her sunken lap and she said, "Will you help me? Will you help me learn him my friend?"

"You want to learn to be friends with God?" I iterated.

"Learn Him my friend. Teach me how. I want to taste the beauty you hold."

I held both of her cold, smooth leathered hands, "You will. You will. I promise." She looked at me in reverence and returned the embrace of my warm hands in hers.

"Thank you," she replied in quiet appreciation.

"I'll keep you in my prayers, Agnes. We will speak again soon!" I assured.

For nearly three months as spring came into bloom, we met several times per week and we talked about God. We read the Bible and I learned how to knit colorful scarves – albeit not well, and my family will not see the fruits of my labor in that craft any time soon. I learned that she grew up in Germany, her husband's life had ended in combat service, and her two stillborn children were the closest she ever got to knowing or needing God before we met. Her life was tragic, yet still hopeful, and my noticeable loneliness on that cold January day had resulted in an unlikely friendship we shared as we softened each other's hearts. On a misty day in early May, Agnes passed away and in mourning her empty chair in the coffee shop the following morning, I experienced God's presence tapping me on the shoulder to remind me that His affirming presence is all that we need. I remember thinking to myself in a quietly elated confidence, *"Aggie met Jesus! I just know it!"* *'Everyone who calls on the name of the Lord will be saved' (Romans 10:13).*

Agnes bestowed me with the honor of writing her obituary after she died and the tapestry of her life I desired to weave with my pen just as eloquently as the art I had watched her create every day. Art that I was also graciously gifted with the week before she passed. For, in the single zipper pocket inside my triathlon bag, I still keep the small, personalized cross she knitted for me. Every time I pack my bag for a race, I reunite with the spirit I knew in her as the soft edges of that cross remind me to have mercy on myself, to give love to others, and to *carry the cross* now and all the way through the finish line.

*"My goal is that they may be encouraged in heart and united in love, so that they may have the full riches of complete understanding, in order that they may know the mystery of God, namely, Christ, in whom are hidden all the treasures of wisdom and knowledge."*

Colossians 2:2-3

# PART IV: FINISHING STRONG

## PERFECTION IS A FALLACY
*The Race Is the Journey*

Recently I was searching for things to write about. I had lost inspiration, drive, and motivation for the very activity I love the most. I know this block to be a normal occurrence, but I couldn't break it this time and as usual I wasted far too much time trying to figure out why. The only concrete conclusion I was able to come to is that I'm at a point in life of trying to discern meaning, trying to strengthen my faith, and also trying to believe that the reality of who and what I am is much greater than I know it to be. Wrestling with the notion of knowing who I am and what I stand for, I am struggling to translate these things into meaningful work that will grow with time and will ultimately allow me to best serve others with my talents.

Nonetheless, I finally gave into my pride about lacking writing ideas and asked a friend of mine, who also writes, what I should write about. I asked for ideas. I asked for encouragement. I was looking for something that would captivate and confuse me. He delivered. His task for me was to write—"The Perfect Life." He told me to describe what it looks like, who is a part of it, the things I have, all the things I wish I didn't have, the way I envisioned everything to be in "The Perfect Life" or "My Perfect life." He said, "Go. Write it. Write the Perfect Life." I loved this idea and it seemed like the "perfect" challenge. My head was trapped in clouds of regrets, of 'should haves,' 'would haves,' and 'if onlys.' This equated to an excellent task. Imagine! If I could erase all the doubts and wants that I never believed would ever come to fruition, I could create the ideal life!

And so I took to writing. I like to write standing up, so there I stood writing on a notepad on the trunk of my car in blistering heat, no less, for over three hours creating "The Perfect Life." I wrote and wrote and wrote. And then the next day swallowed up in the vanity of an idealized reality, I wrote some more.

I don't actually think all that I wrote is worth any audience's time. It was trivial, fantasized, and redundant. Thus, to spare my reader, the *Spark Notes* version of my perfect life included the following:

- Meeting God and walking with Christ sooner in my life
- Growing up with more friends—being less "smart" and more "cool"
- Lacking insecurities
- Being willing to take risks
- Not having consistent stomach problems and pain
- Knowing romantic love at a younger age
- Experiencing more meaningful relationships
- Being a better friend and more intentionally nurturing friendships
- Loving more, but not giving less
- Venturing out on my own rather than staying home

- Being confident, bold, and acting upon my desire for discovery
- Attaining security in self earlier in life
- Being more intelligent, charismatic, athletic
- Keeping my mom happier and treating her better
- Adopting the humility of my father
- Meeting my grandfather
- College degrees equating great success
- Having a career as a lawyer or screenwriter
- Having a wonderful husband and my own healthy family
- Experiencing work and home life without so much stress
- No feelings of loneliness
- No feelings of being hurt
- No feelings of rejection
- Physical perfection
- Forgiveness
- Loving myself. Yes, loving ME.

I could keep this list going for another page of all the things I found to be locked within my warped imagination that maybe somehow believed such things actually translate to "The Perfect Life." But at the end of my listless scribbling, casting of nets on faded hope, it was past evident that the reality of it is that *perfection* doesn't exist—not in self, not in others, and certainly not in life itself.

However, because I don't have that perfect life I envisioned and I know I never will, sometimes I feel as though I am missing out on some glorified version of a contrived reality. I am left thinking I don't know what I want or what to expect, and I often feel like I don't have a past or a future. "Lost" doesn't even begin to describe it. I remain lonely, but sometimes still afraid to be with others. I am trusting, but ambivalent. I subconsciously give myself to anger while deep down grasping for long-awaited hope. I know that maybe I could have everything, yet somehow I feel like I want nothing.

After reading the script about "The Perfect Life" I had described, I didn't exactly feel satisfied. For one, I was glad that I wrote something. My passion and fire had returned, but in the process I had unveiled the beating truth that was there from the very beginning. It's the simple truth that no matter how much I ramble, fumble with my own emotions and thoughts, I can still say with full confidence that I DON'T want that perfect life. I don't want anything to do with it because it's a cynical lie. It's the forced smile on the person shrouded by sadness. It's the clown's face without the costume. It's the Facebook feed that only shows the goading selfies and joy-filled events, but neglects to reveal the tragic story beneath it all.

Following about a week of letting "The Perfect Life" simmer in my thoughts, I reported to my friend that I had written. I thanked him for his suggestion. He asked how it went and he was glad I took his advice. After all, he did get me writing again.

I expressed my gratitude and I explained to him that I didn't produce anything of publishable quality during the last week, but I gained something far more valuable. What I received was a new perspective on everything I once thought I understood. And that is simply that we can't understand it all. We are not supposed to. There is no such thing as a "perfect" life. But what does make it "perfect" are all the things that make it not so. After it's all been written, said, done, and redone, learning what makes life beautiful is actually knowing and accepting ALL of it—each and every one of its imperfections and finding fulfillment in those things. "The Imperfect Life." That's the story we all have the opportunity to write. Go live it. Love it. And make the most of it.

*"Since, then, you have been raised with Christ, set your hearts on things above, where Christ is seated at the right hand of God."*

Colossians 3:1

~~~~~~~~~~~~~~~~~~~~~~~~~~~~~~~~~~~~~~~~~~~~~~~

# YOU'RE STRONGER THAN YOU THINK
*Believe This!*

*"The LORD is my strength and my defense; he has become my salvation. He is my God, and I will praise him, my father's God, and I will exalt him...who is like you— majestic in holiness, awesome in glory, working wonders?"*

Exodus 15:2, 11

In between teaching high school, instructing fitness classes, serving at Church, completing triathlons, running my first half marathon, and cautiously trusting enough to open myself up to new relationships, every day is full. But despite those suppressed tears that sometimes salt my face or the pain that comes from mental and physical fatigue, I'm living a life worth waking up for. Worth smiling for. Worth loving. Because I know I am perfectly made, utterly blessed, and completely loved. I remind myself each day that God's hand is firm and his grasp unfailing.

The author, Ray Bradbury, who wrote my favorite book, *Dandelion Wine*, was a champion of thinking—of truly distancing oneself from life for thought. He claimed the future, with its pace and technology of instantaneous access to information, would prevent deep thought, time for conversations with another, time and SPACE to think. Don't lose that. Find it. Embrace it. Investigate. Challenge yourself. Generate that impeccable idea that has yet to be thought.

Through all of this bafflegab, I suppose what I'm trying to reveal is that I've become content with me. I may not always be ebullient, but I am confident in who I am and who I know I can be. Will there remain days of sadness, of doubt about self-worth, days of criticism or anger? Certainly, that's the guarantee. However, the curtain of steadfast cynicism I once harbored has faded because above all things, I remain happiest in my identity in Christ, and that is a most powerful gift. It has taken me a long time to get to the point of understanding that there's no need for a finite finish line when you're living a life sanctified by God. Yes, I've preached the notion of living this way before, but I've never fully surrendered to it until recently in my life. Perhaps, in so doing, I have acquired a grip on both righteousness and independence. I have stopped concerning myself with what others think and see, and when that narrow lens I have overshadows my life, I remind myself that I'm not living this life for me. There's a greater purpose, and if I dig my heels in now and do the work, the reward will be there. That's the promise and that's also the journey. I'm a slow learner, but I'm getting there. The finish line can wait.

*"God opposes the proud, but gives grace to the humble."*

James 4:6

~~~~~~~~~~~~~~~~~~~~~~~~~~~~~~~~~~~~~~~~~~~~~~~~

# JUST. DO. IT.

Thanks, *Nike*

There's a well-known phenomenon I like to call, "the cult of complacency." It's the very idea that we will generally choose that which requires the least effort, least risk, and most validation. It's choosing what is safe versus what is right and resigning to what is convenient versus that which takes work. It is a debilitating mindset, and it traps the very passions and wants that eat away at our souls each day.

The most difficult part about a race generally is not the actual race itself. It is the commitment to training for it every single day. It is agreeing to make time for the work and the struggle. It is the least convenient decision that there is, but it is worthwhile, holding meaning far greater than your own limited understanding.

I recall being in college several years before I attempted my first triathlon. I was still recovering from my eating disorder, thus knowing my personal limits, and placing those before what I knew I might be capable of doing. A triathlon looked like a thrilling adventure to me, but I knew I could not do it. How could I ever tackle an endurance race when I was not a great runner and I did not have the physical stamina for it? However, I contemplated attempting it for a long time. Gradually, I began learning about average people who completed them, and I decided to start running a few times per week while focusing on my nutrition and working to become a better athlete. I filled my free time reading beginner training plans and following recreational racing guides. For a while, though increasingly intrigued, all I thought was, *Well, that's nice for the other guy—for all of those other people that enjoy this type of thing. That will never be me.*

So I ignored the itch to race, believing in my limitations and letting them set the tone for my life. I told myself despite all odds, "I will never be a triathlete."

Think about it, though. What if I had the same approach to my relationship with Christ? What if I always felt defeated because I was the only one holding myself back? What if I said, "Well, I guess God is for other people because I am not good enough for Him." Actually, I will be honest in that I have said and thought that very thing. In many ways I feel I am unworthy of His love and undeserving of His grace. Fortunately, though, that is not the case. Despite the inability to always dismiss feelings of unworthiness, I know in my heart that God is always there waiting, wanting, and desiring that relationship with us. It is our responsibility to commit to it, to seek it out, and to want to have it in our lives. A training plan for Christ? Absolutely. We are always growing, always learning, and always stretching our faith in newly profound ways towards the eternal promise of life with Him.

A few years of learning about competitive racing passed for me as I remained in that self-defeating mindset where the idea of competing in a triathlon was being minimalized by pestering, debilitating, and self-suffocating beliefs that I could not do it. I recall, though, that one day in prayer—while walking Chip and Dale, my two black-and-white Tibetan Terriers at the time, watching their tails wag with vigor towards a new day and a new park to walk in—I felt God speaking to me telling me that I was good enough, strong enough, worthy enough for anything—from competing in a triathlon to welcoming any challenge faced in life. As I walked in reflective thought, I came to know what I should have known and believed in all along: I can do it! And I am the only one standing in my way.

Later that same evening as I was thanking God, I found myself in an athletics store glancing at polychromatic, overly priced running shoes carrying a slogan that said, "Just do it." I read it again. A slogan I had seen at least one hundred times before: Just do it. I am still giving all glory to Christ for His leadership in my life, but I have some kudos to spread on Nike's behalf. Just do it. Maybe it will be hard. Okay, I know it will be hard. But it was going to be worth my effort, my time, and my commitment.

I decided to buy those funky colorful shoes (once they went on sale, of course), and a few days later signed up for my first triathlon—a race to take place along Lake Michigan in Chicago. I committed to a training plan, and kept up a resilient pace from there. Since then, I have competed in over fifty difference races ranging from triathlons and 5Ks to 10Ks and marathons. Granted, when I signed up for that first race I was scared to death. I was not a runner, was not very muscular at the time, and despite my former abilities in athletics, I did not have a body suited for the challenge. But I dedicated myself to the race and went out and did it. I became my own cheerleader each and every step of the way. For this I am proud, but as anyone who has willed themselves towards achievements once thought unattainable, I do my best to remain humble about overcoming this hurdle and the myriad of other self-doubts encountered in life.

Nevertheless, the point is: the only way to get to the starting line of any race is to just go out and do it! Commit, believe, and find your pace. Surpass your strong. Run your race!

*"Therefore we do not lose heart. Though outwardly we are wasting away, yet inwardly we are being renewed day by day. For our light and momentary troubles are achieving*

*for us an eternal glory that far outweighs them all. So we fix our eyes not on what is seen, but on what is unseen, since what is seen is temporary, but what is unseen is eternal."*

2 Corinthians 4:16–18

# ACKNOWLEDGEMENTS

This book is dedicated to all of the formative mentors, leaders, teachers, grandparents, and friends who laid the foundation for my love of Christ. For it is in the endurance of our faith—our steadfast trust and belief in His will—and our desire to seek and serve the Kingdom of Christ that we are given eternal hope in the reminder of His everlasting love for us.

To my mother and father, Jane and Peter Cladis, who welcomed me into the body of Christ, believed in me, supported me, and inspired me to follow his word, still pray for me daily, and help me to trust in Christ's plan for my life above all things.

To my younger sister, Stacey Cladis, whom I credit most with helping me to overcome a life-threatening eating disorder through showing me Christ's love in the flesh.

To my older brother, Dennis Cladis, for his dependable, unyielding wisdom and guidance as a man of God, and a pillar of faith in my life.

To my fiancé, Matthew Hodge, for demonstrating the selfless love of Christ through his actions and consistent affirmations of others.

To my dedicated friend, Benjamin Dumbacher, for his unwavering friendship in all things. From teaching me the true meaning of fellowship in Christ, giving me the ability to embrace humor, showing me how to make time for the margins of life, to sharing our creative writing endeavors over the years, and of course, for introducing me to the lyrical genius of Bob Dylan—thank you!

And because if I don't include her—she might smite me from heaven—to my Greek grandmother, my ever-lovely Yia-Yia, who never stopped encouraging me to write, to keep writing, and to chase my dreams. I hope she is wearing purple in all its royalty and looking down from heaven with humble pride.

*"Whatever you do, work at it with all your heart, as working for the Lord, not for human masters, since you know that you will receive an inheritance from the Lord as a reward. It is the Lord Christ you are serving."*

Colossians 3:23-24